Other titles in the UWAP Poetry series (established 2016)

Our Lady of the Fence Post by J. H. Crone

Border Security by Bruce Dawe

Melbourne Journal by Alan Loney

Star Struck by David McCooey

Dark Convicts by Judy Johnson

Rallying by Quinn Eades

Flute of Milk by Susan Fealy

A Personal History of Vision by Luke Fischer

Snake Like Charms by Amanda Joy

Books by Alan Gould

Poetry
Icelandic Solitaries
Astral Sea
The Pausing of the Hours
The Twofold Place
Years Found in Likeness
Formerlight (Selected Poems)
Momentum
Mermaid
Dalliance & Scorn
A Fold in the Light
The Past Completes Me – Selected Poems 1973–2003
Folk Tunes
Capital

Fiction
The Man Who Stayed Below
The Enduring Disguises
To the Burning City
Close Ups
The Tazyrik Year
The Schoonermaster's Dance
The Lakewoman
The Seaglass Spiral
The Poets' Stairwell

Essays
The Totem Ship
Joinery and Scrollwork – A Writers' Workbench

Alan Gould

Described by Peter Pierce as 'one of the most intelligent, versatile and elegant Australian writers of his generation', Alan Gould is the author of twenty-five titles, novels, poetry and essay collections.

Of English-Icelandic background, he lived on garrisons in various parts of the world until coming to Australia in 1966. Since 1972 he has been an author as full-time as resources have allowed, he has served on the Literature board of the Australia Council, and represented Australian poetry at events in Manila, Struga and Lincoln (UK).

His literary prizes include the Grace Leven Prize for Poetry in 2006, the NBC Banjo Award for Fiction in 1992, Foundation of Australian Literature Book of the Year (1985), Philip Hodgins Memorial Medal for Excellence in Literature (1999), and co-winner in both The Courier-Mail Book of the Year and ACT Book of the Year in 2001. His 2009 novel, *The Lakewoman*, was shortlisted for the Prime Minister's Fiction Award. His most recent novel is *The Poets' Stairwell* (2015).

Alan Gould
Charlie Twirl

Sixty-one New Poems

First published in 2017 by
UWA Publishing
Crawley, Western Australia 6009
www.uwap.uwa.edu.au

UWAP is an imprint of UWA Publishing
a division of The University of Western Australia

This book is copyright. Apart from any fair dealing
for the purpose of private study, research, criticism
or review, as permitted under the *Copyright
Act 1968*, no part may be reproduced by any process
without written permission.
Enquiries should be made to the publisher.

The publisher wishes to thank *Quadrant, The
Canberra Times, Best Australian Poems 2014* and
2015, The Australian, Southerly. St Mark's Review.
The epigraph for 'Matron' is taken from Ted Hughes'
poem, 'Song For A Phallus' from *Crow*.

Copyright © Alan Gould 2017
The moral right of the author has been asserted.

National Library of Australia
Cataloguing-in-Publication entry:

Creator: Gould, Alan, 1949– author.
Charlie Twirl / Alan Gould.
ISBN: 9781742589268 (paperback)
Australian poetry—21st century.
Ballads.
Folk songs.
Festschriften.

Designed by Becky Chilcott, Chil3
Typeset in Lyon Text by Lasertype
Printed by Lightning Source

Many of the poems in this book take the key for their composition from music, some from traditional folk-song, some from Bach, Dvorak, Sibelius, but most often from Vaughan Williams, (signified as RVW in the text). My interest is that elusive idea of what it is we 'see' in the mind's eye further to the auditory sensations when a piece of music arrests us.

Contents

Making Lines While Listening To Music **10**
Ten Homages To Vaughan Williams
   When Violin Inveigles Air **11**
   A Running Set **13**
   Glissando From A Violin **15**
   A Sublime **16**
   A Morris Jig **18**
   Softly On The Water **20**
   Holy Song **21**
   For Anne, Oboe And Strings **22**
   Fantasia For Tuba **23**
   Romanza **24**
Mercutio Went Through The Veil **25**
An Elephant In The Tuba **27**
It's Bird Week **28**
Stanzas For My Insects **29**
Where Body Believes And Mind Is Blank **31**
Cat-minding **32**
Chat With The Whitest Cat **34**
Addressing The Handicap **35**
When Summer Rains **36**
Spring Song **38**
So If You Know My Inmost **40**
Charlie Twirl **43**
The Insistent Face To Face **45**
On The Beach With Robert Graves **47**
The Epochs Must Go Chatterbox **49**
A Quibble For William Blake **51**
Yeats **52**
Shakespeare **53**
Dream Ballad **54**
The Archaeology Of Southwark **56**
The Poetry Competition At East Choker **57**

Fable: The Ogre Told The Poets **58**
Ready Or Not **59**
The American **61**
A Somerset Rhapsody **63**
Bach's Partita For Violin **65**
For The Finns of 1939 **66**
Two Pomegranates Blush Like Mars **67**
Tonight's Scotch **70**
'Go To Sea No More' **73**
Captain Armchair **75**
The Pauper And the Billionaire **76**
And We Had Hands **77**
Her Lovely Stepping Out **79**
Maidenly **81**
Flambeau! Flambeau! **83**
Lucas Windfall **85**

Tudor Song **86**
Lucas In The Firebox Glare **87**
Lucas Dogfox and The Violin **88**
Inis Oirr **89**
Fiddle Music **90**
Getting The French **92**
Getting The Latin **93**
Matron **95**
Athlete's Foot, 1960 **97**
We Boomer Boys **98**
Titanium Where My Hipsters Rub **100**
Kindling The Real Estate Pages **101**
O Ignis Spiritus **103**

Making Lines While Listening To Music

I was your long-haul poet, I composed
by matching how my hemispheres disclosed
their grainy footage with their clefs of sound
which then I'd fret till happy with their round.

Then came this music, lackadaisical,
and I learned how promiscuous was morale.
Paraap parp-parp, and so on with a tweedle,
here was the flirt where solo horn could sidle

from nearby strings to promptly thrill my joy
that beggared none, nor wow'd a hoi polloi.
Here was such instantaneous effect
upon my snagged, unhappy intellect,

seamed with heartbreak, yet finger-sorcery
to take my fret and make it rhapsody.

> *For music neither pleads nor asks*
> *in its airy arabesques,*
> *will leave no footprint and no husk*
> *and all its ventures are high risk.*

Ten Homages To Vaughan Williams

1. *When Violin Inveigles Air*
('The Lark Ascending')

    Shied by the brute of England
      when I was seventeen,
I've wondered since if a violin
    might come as go-between

to intercede *pro patria*,
    uplift me for those shires
of wooden stiles and Queen Anne's lace,
    and bloodshot-eyed esquires,

    whose farmhands in serge jackets
      belted with baling twine,
went pheasanting in dew-wet fern,
    trousered in cellophane,

and tractors made earth's corduroy
    where diesel and soil ran sweet,
creating abstract canvases
    from corn and sugar beet

    in country gone quadrangled,
      mapping history's work
where slants of sun today are ranged
    to find *this* meadowlark

that scales on strings of light to own
 my self's inchoate part,
where mind takes both the here and now
 to sound their counterpart

in evanescent shires that lume
 with what a music meant
when violin inveigled air
 with shy presentiment.

2. *A Running Set*
(from the RVW of that title)

Bassoons send bees between the trees,
    a shoulder catches sun,
and someone needs her dropped chemise
    if she can be outrun.

'I do not need my dropped chemise.
    I cannot be outrun,
for shapeliest of bumblebees,
    I run so If and Soon

disport themselves at brinks of choice
    where lively is the dance
with all who ever could rejoice
    in their insouciance.'

'If you disport beside a creek,
    what if a damsel-fly
should pause to arch its fine physique
    and ask the question why ...

... *Why am I here, why are you You?*
    Is Why the same as How?
Is Being just a bright bijou?
    And can I call you thou?'

'The bracelets on a damsel-fly
    glow blue and scintillant,
and brute the rules they satisfy
    yet I am nonchalant,

blow hey for muddle, hey for Soon,
while little dogs play peek-a-boo.
A violin pursues the moon
    and I play catch with you.'

3. Glissando From A Violin

('The Charterhouse Suite')

Glissando from a violin
provides the absence I am in,
alighting me on lawn or stone
as though my being had no bone,

where now a debonairing cello
recovers presence for some fellow
who steps out, portly and urbane,
as inward fiddle keeps him sane,

yet will not zero on his place,
will fix no harum-scarum face,
but stirs his presence to such sway,
elides what's here with what's away.

So I live in presentiment
and tease these feints that come half-meant
along vibrations in the air
to ultrasound my everywhere.

4. *A Sublime*
(the Margaret Price solo from 'The Pastoral Symphony')

As though her O
  were auroral swell,
   as fine to earth as
    soul-tissue, to flow
     in the deep interval
      between a molecule
       and a molecule, she airs
        this, awes this, for she's
       a-stream in vowel, in
      vowel's seamless fibre, O
     quavered exhalation
    from a stub pencil's
   uplift into aria, into
             O-finds-O,
    and O her liquidity,
   her ur-genius
    to rise to this somehow,
     this blue elation
      from our pre-noun, from
       our pre-orchestral
        hold on Whole
         on Real, an O-waver
          where old Ralph, old
           serenity meadowed
            in fustian at its,
             wisest ear for joy,
               pencils the vowelled human,

finding singularity,
a tendril out of null,
a sonar meniscus so
local and exquisite
to transcend our air.

5. A Morris Jig
(from 'The King Cole Suite')

When bees went gloved in petals
and trees were green with medals,
we came upbeat and stately
with click of sticks and curtsey,

being Moorish in your English
when the chic of court turned quick
as we danced the roads from London
to the Shires of Workingfolk

on holy days from anvil
and holiday from shovel,
wearing Sunday best with ribbons,
goon hats of plaited straw,

to lose the dark of workshops,
and steely null of dawns
for this our hour of sunlight
where our tattoo steps might sign

the commons of enchantment
to light a spellbound place,
where the long face was the merry
and one camped outside one's face

in the carefree of cared footwork
and our clicked geometry,
where bees worked in their sweatshops
and the trees wore finery.

6. *Softly On The Water*

(from 'Six Studies in English Folk Song')

    The cello finds the dragonfly.
It swerves and stalls like ego in a dream
until piano's slicked liquidity
    uncoils the cognac of a stream,

    where dragonfly must hold its poise,
electron fury in our summer airs,
while this melisma easily alloys
    a wow-and-yes that holds our ears,

    where Being gives its feral *Yes*
to how a pool of air, commodiously
is brought to pitch and then must deliquesce
to turn our mundane instants into spree.

7. Holy Song
(from RVW's arrangement of Psalm 34, 'O Taste and see ...')

   I'm lonely as that fly
      above the map of Europe,
that knows there's scarce one other fly
      sharing this quantum syrup.

   Can I pick carbon bias,
      molecules shy as smiles,
going broad on curves of space,
      heedless of all meanwhiles,

   secreting fatty acids
      encoded with encores
that permeate my membranes where
      new Being opens doors?

   A choir dreams pure tune,
      the cosmos is its doodle,
and every puzzle in that air
      has Being as its middle.

8. For Anne, Oboe And Strings
(from 'The Oboe Concerto')

When air is made it claims no architecture.
These strings and oboe quicken emptiness,
finding the pulse and shape of air's conjecture
to flood it with their momentary excess,

say oboe rousing weather in a house
where plums and ginger cook upon a stove,
and oboe-flow comes seeking where black puss
and newlywed Anne/Alan doze *en rêve,*

while violins insinuate a green
that equally is peace between the stars.
How does an air decide its darling mean?
What shiver turns what's me to what is ours

where you are dark with curls and new with child,
and Queanbeyan air is lithe with oboe scaled
exactly for the scent in dream that comes
from stewing ginger, honey, greengage plums?

9. Fantasia For Tuba
(from 'The Tuba Concerto')

Tuba growl your self possession,
burly drinker give us proof
our merriment is intercession
of quiet word and belly laugh.

Tuba amble down our lanes,
make melody from pools and ruts,
recruit us for some green Cockaigne,
with your longwinded ifs-and-buts.

For, trumpet major, we're at ease
if you'll snore what you think you are
when violins and cellos tease
your solos with their pert hurrah.

Yes, take your vowelled baritone
to brilliant tremolos upon
electrons humming in the stone,
the quiet bow-wave of a swan.

For John 'The Tuba' Falstaff nods
his riotous, endearing head,
affirms the warble of the gods
blows Tuba for its thunderhead.

10. *Romanza*
(from 'The Tuba Concerto II')

    One cello from its couch of sound
    will trail my love's slow wandering
through this, our married air and sunlit place.
    And it can nuance and attend
    the colours of her wondering ...
O yes, but still can't find her lasting face
    which painters, narrowing an eye,
    spontaneously identify.

    Now here comes Raku Pussycat
    to seize his perch by my love's ears,
so both may amble tall from room to room
    and inventory our this-and-that
    like a pair of auctioneers,
and they'll do mischief to the seem and groom
    from melody that finds its space
    by finding ground that has no place.

    Four fingers flickering a stave
    in just that blithe continuum
will strew the human *now* with *furthermore*,
    conjure this merry with this brave
    in my love's presence, yet is stumm
should someone take a box of chalks and draw
    the fine exactness of her cheek,
    when cat and she make one physique.

Mercutio Went Through The Veil

Mercutio went through the veil,
    became a pussycat,
a Siamese, alert and male,
blue-eyed and muscular and trim,
knew his wherein from his whereat ...
    Now we've acquired him.

His fur gleams pale like chinaware,
    we call him Raku Svelte,
courtier of Strut and Tail-in-air,
the friar's bell around his neck
that tingles when he licks his pelt
    or paws a moth on spec.

And mynahs, ganging in our tree,
    with yellow roundel eyes,
find how their zest for oratory
(when Raku Svelte discreetly strops
his claws where they extemporise)
    abruptly stops.

So boyo id burls through our rooms,
    gallop of paws on boards.
What is it in a cat assumes
a human finger idly set
upon an armchair still discords
    like some lewd Capulet?

In small hours, when the frost has spread
    its lacework on our lawn,
this Raku comes to my love's bed
and, lightly touching nose-to-nose
(for courtiers flaunt their right to fawn),
    settles where she allows ...

and through milk-sleep Verona flows
from house to house as both dispose.

An Elephant In The Tuba

I know a dance the elephants believe
Roethke

From here the dapper elephant
    embarks on trot,
whether the brass is eloquent
    or whether it's not.

He rises from these parps,
he's self-possessed as levity,
and has such sober dance-steps
with which to tease Earth's gravity.

Watch for his thoughtful sway,
    le tour à pirouette,
the charm with which he honks hooray
    to Bella or Minette.

In Asia and in Africa
where tubas are mysterious,
this threesome waltz for Nkosi man and vicar,
    and prove they're serious.

It's Bird Week

There's flutter-trill and strut-about as Monday's crested pigeons
provide us the behaviourals for Homer's Greeks and Trojans.

On Tuesday there are bronze-wings with their courtier self-images,
the sun igniting petrol on their epaulettes and plumages.

The mid-week has the mynahs on invisible trapezes,
yellow is their hosiery, unending their *sottises*.

Now Thursday and galahs have come, like Hardy's wives to market.
while cockatoos stand on my lawn like batsmen at a wicket.

We're clubbing on the Friday with the jittery rosellas
who jump up on their bar stools if approached by uncouth fellahs.

Galahs again on Saturday, galahs are half the planet
and each squeaks like a bedspring when there's rhythmic pressure on it.

On Sunday night the frogmouth flies across the hillside silence
dark constable who brings the mice no safety or condolence.

Yet every day presumes a day when dailiness is not,
like when the bower-bird's at gym beneath our apricot,

its one eye blazing at us while its other is elsewhere,
construing Virgil's *Georgics*, annotating Molière.

Stanzas For My Insects

The little moths in capes of velveteen
will dig quick profits from our almond meal.
For these our larder spiders set fine trawl,
    and patience is their scene.
       *

    What do the ants consume,
    fervent along their cables?
And if they sleep, then do they sleep a-swarm,
    blackleather as bibles?
       *

Mosquito, I once heard a pilot say
the nightsky owns 'some Godalmighty space'.
So tell me how, with all that choice, your way
has such exact coordinates for my face?
       *

Black admiral spread your spinnaker
and broad-reach through my quarter acre,
adept at windward ploy and leeward slack,
and then abruptly take yourself aback,
    and hover, all your sails a-shiver,
when citrus trees secrete you something clever.
       *

O silverfish you've found my Freud.
Unconscious Mind is now a void.
So will you next commence on Joyce ...
Will stream-of-consciousness lose voice?

Yes silverfish, you tat exquisite lace
    makes Conan Doyle an awkward case.
    White islands grow where Conrad sailed;
I loved his timbre till his pages failed.
            *

    No dirt is dug, no hint of sleaze
    can taint the single-minded bees.
    Like pollsters going door to door,
these proles know what a blossom sweetener's for.
    With all their solemn hum, like rumour,
what if the bees possessed a sense of humour
    and found the processing of honey
            innately funny?
            *

    My darling showers at 3 a.m.
when peckish daddy longlegs eat their kind.
And in warm rain my darling watches them,
    for she is of enquiring mind.

Our bathroom spiders rarely suffer loss.
    Should one go down the plug,
my love contrives, with dentifloss
    a lifeline for that bug.
            *

Why is my home so insect and imperial
with settlers subterranean and aerial,
like here, this mantis on my window glass,
outlandish twig of prayer? Such gravitas!

Where Body Believes And Mind Is Blank

What lemur code lives in my feet
allows that, if I shed conceit,
I'll rouse that monocycling man
lit high upon my circus wire
who tows his gimcrack caravan
of archive for my heart's desire?

> *To find what code lives in your feet,*
> *don't ever ask, 'Am I complete?'*

When ace possession takes my hands
to follow where my chisel tends
through lambencies of yellow wood
to what is new yet understood,
what email-flash inside my head
has blithed hard rules of A–Z?

> *To make that email web succinct*
> *dissolve all thought of how you're linked.*

I fell from height into my tree,
snatched rescue from its canopy.
Along my track a snake arose
but we exchanged prompt courtesies.
So where's that air in which I travelled?
those facts and spells at which I marvelled?

> *Those spells are one particular,*
> *your earliest and nearest star.*

Cat-minding

(to the tune of 'Hugh The Graeme'; felicitously, accent may drift across either syllable of Béyaz.)

Beyáz the cat has a-hunting gone
by rhubarb stalks and garden sheds,
and sentient stuff he's chanced upon,
with footwork he has torn to shreds.
    Mew and miaow, here's lightning tactics
    Mew and miaow, here's feline tact.

Beyáz the cat is white as talc
and lives in paintings by Magritte.
He purrs with snores as bland as milk ...
'Good pussies play with what they eat.'
    Mew and miaow, here's deep-space whiskers,
    Mew and miaow, here's stately frisk.

Dangle your fingers from a chair,
this Béyaz pussycat is sure
to leap from art's to nature's laws,
man-eating dreams between his claws.
    Mew and miaow, here's fleshy sketchwork,
    Mew and miaow, here's yawn-and-stretch.

He improvises snoring jazz
on my love's wide and talc-white bed,
which is one reason that Beyáz
and I go at it, head-to-head.
    Mew and miaow, here's rival dalliance,
    Mew and miaow, here's eyed locale.

Now Béyaz trots across the lawn,
the laundry dries upon its hoist,
this Monday's bright, my hand untorn,
Magritte's poised squirrel brush is moist.
    Mew and miaow, who's clever pussy?
    Mew and miaow, who's studious?

Chat With The Whitest Cat

Beyáz, you Mùscovite, bliss to your furs,
sprawled at our hearth with its coral *chaleurs*.

Cat are you dreamy where dreams are rehearsals
of cats in their snowdrifts all famished for morsels?

Cat, are your manners unique or sub-lunary?
You taproot in murder then tongue at your finery.

What's season for cats? Can cattishness tremor
in catkins of springtime and catspaws of summer?

There's brass in a samovar brass in your manner,
I call you my pussy yet know you're a loner

to trot in late summer when paddocks are stubble,
when evening has cherried the sun to a bauble,

and small birds must gossip while looting your orchard,
enigma that tears them – deep down are you wretched?

Is heaven of sentience triggered by glimmer.
not prey in its doombox, but prey-*and*-its-glimmer?

Behind your shut eyes are there cats will connect
with all that is white and a-flicker and licked?

Béyaz, you snowfield, here's bliss to your pelt,
most white of your cosmos, both dealer and dealt.

Addressing The Handicap

(for Ms Sushila Likmabum, India's judo finalist at Glasgow Commonwealth Games)

My Christian name's Sushila, my surname's Martyrdom,
I took up sport with just one thought, a surname's overcome
by hurling hopefuls several floors, depending on my mood-Oh.
So here I am, the Indian lamb, and out for Gold in Judo.

My surname is a standing joke around the stadium,
and sniggers ride the coverage across all Christendom.
But I'm a girl can whirl and hurl and never leave a sore bit
for all I've launched contestants from arena into orbit.

Sushila Quick, Sushila Slick, Sushila leaves you stumm.
I'll toss you all round Glasgow and right back to where you're from.
The sun shines in the sky and from another place I'm told.
But I will lick all hopefuls who go down there seeking gold.

When Summer Rains

When summer rains come
 breathing, they free a sunned
 laundry-scent from our tarmac
 as birch leaf and mulberry leaf
 grow greenly quick with such
  demure shiver like pre-sex ex-
 hilaration.
      When summer rainfall
  grows to a saturating noise,
  its fibres slantly astigmatise
  my neighbour's vast peppermint gum,
  while torrent makes smoke along
   the roof-cap of his egg-shell blue
  toolshed.
          When summer downpours
    cellophane my downhill view
     there's science immanent in glassy wires
     grown pale and dense with application,
     so precise is the drag of its descent
     at five degrees aslant our power poles.
     Yet somehow, like a counter-theme,
      O look, as sun now lays a score
      of minims on the squall's pale rift,
      to show how light is quick and deft
      where rain-pools glitter.
                  When rains
         must pelt the biscuit earth, they tweak
         momentarily our asphalt driveway
         with silver pepperpots, while epic
         over New South Wales each tree,
         each molecule and cell, now clicks
         to fine hydraulic protocols.

When summer rains arrive
they take the template of terrain
in thrilling negative.
                When summer rains
go sonar, a drummer's brushwork
scythes and seethes; canopies
curtsey to such soft percussion,
gutters trombone jazz, a downpipe
drips with diamond fullstops.

Spring Song
(to the tune of Tom Moore's 'Fill the Bumper Fair')

Start a fiddle-murmur,
start the fingers pecking,
start a honey rumour
where the bees are working,
Spring has thrown its switch,
all the circuits humming,
frogs possess our ditch,
mynahs at their bombing,

Brownsnake now you cruise
down our paling fences.
Deaf-one do you choose
where your best suspense is?
Spring must meet its quota,
purple flower and joey,
candidate and voter
raising ballyhooey.

Shingleback you shuffle
like a knight in armour.
Do you cop an earful
shuffling with your charmer?
Spring parades the fashion,
girls wear petal dresses,
bonking's in full session,
blossom effervesces.

Bottlebrush has bristled,
scarlet are its dreadlocks,
bikies terse and muscled
earlobes hung with padlocks,
Spring is at its thesis,
rain brings keyboard patter,
season of increases ...
... what's life but pressing matter?

So If You Know My Inmost

And since you've seen the wiles o' me,
Come tell to me your name.
Trad, *The Forester*

    'So if you know my inmost
      why not reveal your name?
For Annabels and Clarabels
    will not be thought the same

by one upfront and forelock boy,
    sleek beside swimming pool,
adroit with pleasantries between
    our sheets of sweet misrule.

For now the dawn has come with broom
    to sweep away the stars
and slip them in her pocket with
    her keepsakes and ménage,

and I am now your data, love,
    yes, your magnetic field,
so since you know my physics, love.
    I'll have your name revealed.'

'Some call me Shy, some call me Shock,
    some call me Scaramouche.
But I'm the chough with crimson eye,
    the bronze-wing in the bush.

Some call me Raindrop-on-a-leaf,
    some call me Hidden Face,
but when I earn my livelihood
    I'm simply known as Ace.'

'Some call you this, some call you that,
    some call you demigod,
but when you're at your workplace, love,
    I know you're Wally Plod.'

He's jumped astride his motorbike,
    he's off across the hill.
On skateboard she's abreast of him
    though still she's deshabille.

She's chased him through the valleys and
    beside the reservoirs,
then down into the city with
    its serpent gleam of cars.

He's in the lift and rising fast
    to Level Forty Four,
but she is in the stairwell and
    arriving there before.

The views are angel views up here
    Hobart to Borneo,
and Daddy's in his swivel chair,
    his hirelings come and go.

    'Big Daddy, here's your flunkey
    who crept below my guard,
but would not give his name to me
    for all he left his card.'

Her daddy gazes through the glass,
    Hobart to Borneo.
Her daddy speaks with quite a growl ...
    'Here's what I think will flow ...

'If Wally has a loving heart,
    but more, a careful ear,
then I foresee there might well be
    the wedding of the year.

'But if he is a fly-by-night,
    a varmint and a shonk
he'll sleep his nights with crabs and mites
    in the slums of Honkytonk.'

Confetti blushed across a scene,
    they're married forty years,
a magnate's only daughter and
    a scamp with careful ears.

Charlie Twirl

16/8/1945 George Street, Sydney

This is the Street of Hullaballoo
when poor link arms with the well-to-do,
two Diggers drunk beyond all help,
vast crowds a-sway like ocean kelp.

This is the Street of Broad Hooray.
Papers blizzard on its grey,
and folk go wigged in shredded files;
unprompted are their camera smiles.

My darlings, look, we have come through!
declare the crowds on Hullaballoo,
who conjure from their one ahoy
this genie now to seize their joy,

to skip and sway and doff his trilby,
pirouette his sideways smile,
and signal how all futures will be
made the lighter for his style.

This is no more than circumstance,
and this tall fellow's brilliant dance
has just eight seconds in our view
as Newsreel trawls on Hullaballoo.

Yet catch the sob of pure release
from those for whom he's centrepiece
so bravo and so fugitive
as he takes flight in 'forty five,

this Mister Zeitgeist, Charlie Twirl –
whose name will be historical
for all there's nothing in a name
when dance outdances personal claim

to touch the quick of what's in view
along the tides of Hullaballoo,
where strangers link an arm and arm
to joy at others saved from harm

on isles of acrid ballyhoo
where wreckage is the homely view
till lifted now from that sheer pall
by this so debonair morale.

Our camera tremors on its scene
to steady light for where we've been,
this day of papers churned to snow
and crowds in archipelago,

to lift us with these ballet motions,
this blithest fuse for huge emotions,
with commentary so bygone, yet
the footage of this pirouette

tracking the shots on Deep Hooray
where this Mad Hatter flaunts his sway,
lighting what's meant when Hullaballoo
slips arm through arm with me and you.

The Insistent Face To Face

At whisky light I scratch my head;
it seems that I'm now sixty five,
reckon live authors who are dead
outnumber dead ones who're alive.
Unreasonable this tyranny
that keeps these from my company.

Say you, Geoff Chaucer, bureaucrat
when poets still went saddle sore,
that teeming world beneath your hat
could not defend you, Councillor,
from being robbed of horse and purse
for all you breathed a Universe.

John Skelton, in your room of birds
where hawk and Philip Sparrow play,
I catch the sheer astonished words
you find for Margáret Husséy
to bring her through our centuries
intact in loveliness and poise.

Tom Wyatt, burly-beard, you stoop
through doors to where a bed is made,
Behind you is the cock-a-hoop
of sexual frenzy's light and shade,
and yet exquisite your *tristesse*,
which brings that girl's 'how like you this?'

Marvell finessing arguments
when argument might save your head
as deftly as it lights good sense
for two to sprint from pew to bed,
and, taking respite from dour hymns,
luxuriate their naked limbs.

So tell me, fellows, how you set
the chairs in fidget round my room ...
What is a poem's *tête à tête*,
its live, inchoate theorem,
will have you breathing in my space,
each poet's insistent face-to-face?

On The Beach With Robert Graves

The wind seeks out the dead whale's ribs –
an earliest lyre that tongues and probes,
and Robert Graves, you're on this beach
to coax a poem into reach,
and I'm here too, to quiz if good
attends a lyric livelihood

when click-and-pluck caress the ear
as shantyman enchants the oar,
when tink, then thump, two hammers hit,
iambic lightning flares from it,
as barefoot, you, with oar and forge,
tickle how English poems emerge.

Robert, you have the deadpan eyes,
that watched gas dawns on Flanders rise,
and saw how war's atrocious farce
infected too that tranche of verse
wherever tawdry jubilee
had spoiled, for you, our art's integrity.

Did no-man's-land prepare your nerve
to deal the shibboleths their serve,
clap Pound and Milton in the stocks
to cop your cabbages and knocks?
Were you unfair? My oath, for all your humour
swims in moral seas with Homer.

Your grandson lived three doors from me,
and shared his grandad's roguery,
shambled our hillside, slicked with sweat
then suddenly was dead from heart,
his big dog, ghostly through our trees,
stampeding twilight's kangaroos.

Two Roberts, barefoot, who compose,
the durance of a family nose,
a burly and endearing *Geist*
that ghosts how likenesses persist.
The same for poems? Might a screen
display a genome for the lyric scene?

And do I write my poems for money?
(their cat-walks cannot tease me any)
Perhaps I write them to be famous
along the broadway of disclaimers.
Or do I not make them at all,
but they write me both large and small

as verbal music thrums a rib,
that Robert, you and I transcribe
in trance, in heartbreak and with toil
to make for other poems their soil,
while anvil, oar and you and me,
make soundings in this charity?

The Epochs Must Go Chatterbox
(after watching Evelyn Waugh on YouTube)

This ailing man's a gentleman
who now lacks purchase on our air,
yet Evelyn Waugh's uptight élan
enlarged the presence of Voltaire
by losing none of Evelyn Waugh.

And here is Henry Fielding deep
in where a moral clowning quickens
for dopey charmers, half asleep,
who mass toward where commerce thickens,
in beehive energies of Dickens.

John Updike hears this badinage;
it comes across the drawing rooms
where Sterne and Smollett are at large.
So Updike doodles genial dooms
to lume where comic buzz resumes.

For epochs *must* go chatterbox.
John Milton talks to William Blake,
so Blake can deal alarum knocks
that bring the dreamy Yeats awake
to take his share of poetry's ache,

while Wyatt tickles Campbell's ear
with 'Whoso list to hunt, I know ...'
that from five centuries appear
those 'cruel girls we loved' who show
their daughter's brilliant counterglow.

And here are Judith Wright's two fires
lit on a hearth that Plato used
to smelt those human ur-desires,
ideal and actual living fused
on flesh that history has bruised.

The singular that is a voice
will find its life from others' sense
exquisitely within a choice
of what will light intelligence
from chat so casual and immense.

A Quibble For William Blake

Fine Tints without Fine Forms,
so Mister B.'s opinion storms,
will always be the subterfuge
of the blockhead and the stooge.

   Yet when that coy Big Bang
     swelled formless like a hot meringue,
say, Mister B. where were the hints
gave Form the premium in your prints,
         not Tints?

   For there's attrition here
between twin variants of human dare,
   and both will take our fancy back
to when we smeared on Altamira rock,
   aeons before the complex saints
distracted us from tell-tale tints and scents,
   got us our lunch, but that's not all,
   showed how the casual and small
   possessed antennae for the whole.

Yeats

'Bred passion against the times, made wisdom strong.'
A.D. Hope

Lucid dandy, curing words
to shoe your dears with skins from birds,
preposterous those haughty loves
candlestick'd in fish-skin gloves ...

Yet who *dare* quiz your mundane wish
to stitch the fabric of a fish
(be it trout or moonlit elver)
that Irish girls might sleeve in silver ...

or walk the leather from a sparrow
in sandals that can warm the marrow
of their exquisite anklebones
on chill Monaro afternoons?

Here was the glint you gave me, William,
from all your wise and headlong bullion ...
that only paltriness in love
could stint my darling trout-skin gloves.

Praise genius that has nous to spree
with reasoned magic for company
such that the madcap and the sane
might *tête à tête* within one brain,

might tit-for-tat this side of sane.

Shakespeare

The Droeshout Portrait

I get this rictus for your face,
high collared Dude.
Where is your warm by which we punters press
on you some gratitude

when on my fingers
the leather smell of Iago lingers,
and Falstaff, burling from a tune,
inhabits light I call my own?

Here Bardolph squints,
here Shylock dabs some fussy scents,
and these come natural on my street,
escape your little whiskers when we meet.

O you had knack
to find iambic yakkity yak
could pinion how morale might curl and pulse
to limn a self with all its else.

I praise your sense
to seize on each intelligence,
and from their sum make ground where I belong,
your scrutiny so sidelong.

Dream Ballad

Last night I dreamed I merely died
then walked with Shakespeare at my side.
His vivid people were in view,
but smaller now like residue.

We two were easy, one-to-one
as though from single dust undone,
and in this ultra likelihood
we took all past as understood,

and spoke of loves when we grew fond
on by-ways that were *demi-monde*,
and how, to prompt a truelove's laugh,
was to unveil a better half,

where love was magma, solar flare,
yet also numen of not-there.
'If I loved her and she loved me
where was the edge of entity?'

We live, my dream-companion said,
*within some now of watershed
where all my darlings chased their good,
both true and phoney through my wood.*

*And some adored what they despised,
and some came early, some disguised,
and some were children, bodies lit,
outgrowing papa's rule and wit*

to find such nuanced moral round
must bring them to their killing ground.
Now all my darlings make a whole
that in one atom would be small.

'Can I show proof I loved,' I asked,
'now Anne lives on while I am masked?'
(My Shakespeare was a watchful man,
gamekeeper's eye for how love ran).

"I walked my truelove through your trees
where we lacked lovers' expertise;
there was no wood before she came
when each new thing appeared the same.

I walked my truelove where the lees
of sunlight lit the canopies.
We badinaged and sometimes fought.
Joyous the dailiness days brought."

I told him this in that no-place
where being was adrift from face.
We had no path, yet knew the way,
and could forestall what each might say.

For we were easy and innate
and all our living inchoate.
Can we show proof we loved? he smiled.
When dust and thought grow reconciled.

The Archaeology Of Southwark

(after reading my son's honours thesis in archaeology)

We're dusting *posset* bowl and *albarello* jar
to air sub-landish shards of what we both once were,
unsheathing centuries from cake-of-river slime
to welcome folk we thought were duly lost to time,
that we might come ourselves more whole to earth and Time.

So what comes clear in nook and coign of English words?
Can I bring *posset*-milk or *posset*-ale to curdle
within the cipher archive of these jigsaw shards?
Does sugar kick here still? Does cinnamon still dawdle
to tang an understairs where Kit and Joan canoodle?

And 'albarello' – catchword that mongrel ears import,
this cream majolica from Tuscan druggists' shelves
to make ceramic sheen vibrate in English thought,
to detail finely every tile we call 'ourselves',
bring otherness of others that we might find ourselves.

Because we must, we pick the mind's exquisite layers
to conjure Tudor faces, cheerful or distraught,
and argue their persistence in our lives like lawyers
refiguring smallest shards to make a case for court,
and here's both shard and word, the lumen that we court.

The Poetry Competition At East Choker

(... your forbearance, TSE)

So here we are, poets in the middle way,
also-rans in a local poetry encouragement
where 'to win' insinuates the customary ignominy
from co-opted mind tasked with annual duties.
Journeymen, do we not inhabit an important city,
moiled in our era's rage for the mediocre
where stale peevishness sighs at aspirational words
claimant upon their hours and *caritas?*
                                        ... O mate,
do we not learn only to navigate
the choppy shallows of confused agenda,
agenda verily subverting our credible flair
with their prosaic consideration, preventing our brilliance
with a native necessity to see that art
may persist in penitentiary light?
                                 ... O mate,
for us remains only the sighing,
this fitting-up is not our business.

Fable: The Ogre Told The Poets

The ogre told the poets they could make
each ego-smear their artwork for his sake.
   That was his slavery
   for which they volunteered.
   Wearing that livery
   proved their sole reward.

Compliance meant their efforts all were geared
to gravel local strangeness from each word
the while the ogre watched them, undeterred
by how each pleaded art's integrity,
   and smiled as they careered
toward his trash heap where all work's absurd.

Ready Or Not

(a skip tune)

Jump, jump, ready or not!
Your bro is in the doghouse,
your daddy is a nut.
Jump, jump, know you're alive
both now and in nineteen fifty-five.

At some still point of '50's toddlerhood
I watched the agile fingers of Miss Wood
mint piano notes to flood our dour school hall,
then strew them tumbling in their free-for-all.

She lined us up and had us sing a song.
Is tunelessness a kind of moral wrong?
She poised her ear beside my churning bouche
tilted her pretty eyebrow, bade me hush.

Sing, sing, you're out of key!
Your daddy is a chimpanzee,
And you must feel you're one-of-the-crowd ...
But Sweet, don't speak that need too loud.

The pipers surged from childhood like a wave
their kilts and sporrans swaying like sea-kelp,
drum-major hurling high his gleaming stave,
and *petit-moi* too drowned in skirl for help.

First music here, the musketry of drums,
bass drummer apron'd in his leopard skin,
and pipers with their urgent sonar plumes
creating turmoil that my life was in.

Coming, coming, ready or no.
Your hidey-holes are where you'll grow.
Here's Mister Snot behind the door,
some petit moi who's sixty-four!

The American
(from the Dvorak, String Quartet)

His cello spoke to violin,
   Now tilt me something new
will light me to that vowelled within
   beyond where words construe.

His fiddle was a diplomat,
   made nuance finely where
aristocrat went slantwise at
   the common people's fare.

I'll nimble you a melody
   where pollen takes the warm
and trout hang in gold lethargy
   below where gnats perform.

I'll spiral you sheer mountain walls
   where snow lifts off like smoke.
I'll nuance old world rigmaroles
   of dancing gentlefolk.

A blue bird filled the canopy,
   a green bird sang below.
He could not be in Tennessee
   till music made it so.

A hillside found its violin,
   a cello held its shire
where trees, as green as apple skin,
   were taking orange fire.

A cirrus prairie overhead,
    he walked in Idaho
in some inchoate blessed instead
    when music made it so.

The charmed musician, dropped his score
    to join that further dance
where words dissolve their metaphor
    into insouciance.

A Somerset Rhapsody

(Gustav Holst composing, Yehudi Menuhin on violin)

Mmmenuhin, Menuhin,
the bees are at their orchard din
and I will catch that pure élan
from your eliding violin,
to go down into Somerset
and relocate a scuttle butt
of my North Curry kin,

where John Gould with his first moustache,
can not yet write his name when asked,
but puts big feet to canny use
when fiddle tunes are fast and loose.
And Lizzie Clifford with long face
twirls circumspectly in that place
with Hannah, William, Anne and Ben,
washerwomen, husbandmen.

For Gustav Holst has tuned his ears,
to pick grave dance steps from the years
and turn them into lures of sound
that draw my dead from underground,
great grandpa and great grandma both,
sepia'd in their dark broadcloth,
my forbears on a parish roll
who did not doubt they owned a soul.

Menuhin, Menuhin,
sighting down your violin,
I'll catch the uplift and the tweedle
that draws the frolic from the fiddle
where John Gould dances chin to chin
with Lizzie Clifford who will get
his awkward mind with alphabet,
that stern and steady-gazing dame
who turned his black marks to a name,

but now takes crotchets to be merry
beside the Levels of North Curry
that Menuhin, Mmmmenuhin
has conjured with his violin
where the bees are at their din.

Bach's Partita For Violin

I stopped to hear a fiddle argue
arithmetic with immanence,
to see what their dispute might augur,

and learned how fiddles do not wrangle,
but fancy, with a child's persistence,
liquidity in dance with angle,

how horsehair trying tautened strings
locates that further reach of sense,
will find the air's mathematics sings,

and this Old Wig with red-rimmed eyes
notating snails of consequence
to try, where bread-and-butter lies,
his calculus for paradise.

For The Finns of 1939

(Sibelius, Karelia Suite).

Sibelius was our good, for all our odds were real and bad;
they flew some forty aeroplanes for every one we had.

They camouflaged themselves for earth, we wore to match the snow.
That Winter War was roadless war except the Road to Woe.

Bottled petrol down a hatch, a crowbar jammed in tracks,
one human nerve will stop a tank when need and music mix.

Your sniper is a lover for he courts the one-on-one.
Beware the purpose where good conscience cannot be undone.

Our trumpets touched Karelia, our drums soughed metaphor.
We lost our few too often, but we cost the Boris more.

Who wins a winter war? Not us, though we staked our 'Hereby'.
There's spoiled faces in the snow. Sweet music tells you why.

Two Pomegranates Blush Like Mars

Two pomegranates blush like Mars,
where butterflies now intervene
like graph lines on our olive green,
data for dreaming as I doze
in this alignment of my stars
where my good luck outstrips my woes.

Anne Langridge put this garden here.
She built and stucco'd yellow walls,
then placed pistachios, that their wiles
of male and female tree might flirt
along the pathways of my near.
How can cell-frenzy seem inert?

With shells like well-kept fingernails,
pistachio nuts will turn to pink,
and I know I get space to think
in gardens free from enmity
for all the crimson parrot males
glare down from our black mulberry tree

when I have placed my ladder there
to steal the breakfast from milords,
two livelihoods that lack accords.
My periwinkle berries drop
into this scarlet bucket where,
(for now) the human claim's on top.

And good-willed folk have sent my screen
footage of Paris youths who ply
their clubs and rage on passers-by,
and this is done to have me learn
I can no longer choose between
the enmities with which they burn.

A hammer-hit, a Paris girl
curls like a foetus on the ground ...
My YouTube mutes her plaintive sound
to let the commentator talk
us through this routine Paris whirl
where hitters in their hoodies walk.

I have been married to my girl
for three decades-and-more that muss
the brush of skirts around our house,
and times of kids and jollity
that speed us to that vortex whirl
will ash her *this*, will dust this *me*.

How do I know what value is
when I lack time to know our whole?
Is there a viewpoint that can tell
the worth that love and love may find
beside the flexing galaxies
that make themselves remote from mind?

I love this girl, and from her learn
how nonchalant, a laugh or glance
will claim some underpinning dance
my colder mind will not accept.
If I have mind, how do I earn
the further view by which I'm rapt

while wrapped in days fanatics use
to terrorise some innocent
until their blink-of-spite is spent?
Two pomegranates blush like Mars,
I learn what has and lacks excuse,
and how worth stands among the stars.

Tonight's Scotch

Consider the lilies of the field, how they grow;
They toil not, neither do they spin.
(Matt 6:28)

Tarpaper hobos – holed socks in kip beneath –
    your faery rises to my nose
       from this, my emptied whisky glass.
When beggars go a-dream they bare their teeth,
    but I have not been one of those
for all my fancy can enact their case.

How close can any inner seeing run
    to catch a living not its own
       from whisky hints ... or spider thread
that glints in zephyrs from our steady sun?
    Is most far-thinking done alone
on spindle light as tenuously shed?

Along my autumn hillside kangaroos
    will stand alertly as I pass.
       A doe will take a fobwatch, note
how here's a stroller lacking nostril clues,
    to pose as rival for her grass.
Here's livelihood that copes without a vote.

And here's a scrawl on cardboard and a beard
    who begs my alms at supermart.
       I've come here to spend big on cheese,
will give no coins to see this voter cheered,
    because I reason larger heart
insists a fellow stir his faculties.

Sell all you've got, and give it to the poor,
    and here's a beard and crumpled cap,
      contemptible, yet no less real
than any voter feral at my door
    on some behalf to ease mishap.
What is the ground where Beard and I might deal?

Not coins. Coin is addictive charity.
    I knew a trainee doctor once,
      a Scot who took each beggarman
and sat the fellow down to cakes and tea.
    He would not give those pockets pence,
gave time instead, and patient man-to-man,

and did the good because it found him able.
    This beard stares at his inner crux
      as nearby buskers caterwaul
their conscience-sonar, finding hook and bible
    to pause the shopping crowd and tax
some trick of livelihood into a bowl.

And lilies of the field send out their good
    on tendril toil-and-spin to find
      their chances from soil-expertise
and trick a planet's trove of likelihood.
    Is this so different in its kind
from voters scouting shelves for fancy cheese?

Tarpaper tramps, and that astounding man
    above the lilies of his field
    who drew a new imagining
between the winner and the also-ran,
    and looked to lives that were unsealed
under the dark that is our given thing.

'Go To Sea No More'

'*There goes Jack Strapp the poor sailorlad*
He must go to sea once more.'
Trad, Go To Sea No More

Svelte liquor was my lightning, and here again was I
resilient like a lichen on the inside of my spree,
a Jack sworn-off already going chatterbox and flirt,
with brand new fobwatch, weskit, and crisp-as-shop white shirt.

For who'll forbear to babble when the amber liquid croons
like comely Ma's excuses for the hardcase of her sons?
And me all for dry livelihood, my money new that morning
from fifteen months of ocean-work, my sweetest nature yearning.

But I was steered up staircase, and on a pillow smeared –
Did Angie have a bosom or did Angie have a beard?
I knew I had a fobwatch and banknotes thick as leather
but Angie knew how pockets brought improvements to her weather.

I cried, I hoped to die, indeed the best of me played dead.
But kindly, cackling whores were light to lead me from that bed.
'Jack Strapp, Jack Strapp, you'll find no lap, when lightning is your mother.
You know the soak and drear of ships. Now go and find another.'

There's liners trimmed with fancy lights like bubbles in champagne.
My head lay on a packing case, tarpaper kept off rain.
There's freighters do quick passages, hot dinners in their holds.
and shirts as crisp as snow provide thin cover from the cold.

I'd like to be a shopkeeper, range tins along a shelf,
I'd like to be a factory hand with time-off for myself.
But I got sent to Davis Strait to use a flensing knife,
and grew so cold to Life I did not want to own a life.

The white comes off grey skylines there as chill as any blade.
I'd rather be a cattleman who warms a dairymaid.
A whale will thrash its blood to liquor in them Greenland fjords.
I'd like to be a svelte milord, spend more than life affords.

Captain Armchair

When I was Skipper Armchair and I set a broad topgallant,
I sent aloft the numbskull boys and those with rising talent.
My seaboots tilted round your world, I cosied to my binnacle
and close-hauled past Cape Fantasy, gave sea-room to Cape Cynical.

The estuaries I called at were alive with virtual ships,
and the lighters came in-tow across the moonlight's water-lips,
to bring us cargoes with their smells of coal or coriander,
and seasoned crews undone by shore, still snoozing from some blinder.

So what's a cringle, what's a splice, and what's the view from high
at orange dawn when loosing sail, departing from Shanghai?
My name is Captain Armchair and I'm strangely twice alive,
for all life grows uneasy when two livings must connive.

Now buntlines are all unbelayed and gimbals bang my brain,
and futtock shrouds go fraying on what was pure fancy's main.
Now rocker gear clanks cable over greasy windlass pawl,
and I have heard the shanty-stuff converted to pop drawl.

When I was Skipper Armchair and my limits were the planet
I'd take a ship wherever there were nouns and verbs to man it.
When lexicons unloosed their sails and sheave-pins squeaked with strain
to work to windward of the real was compass for my brain.

The Pauper And the Billionaire

A million years beside their fire
the pauper and the billionaire
were silhouettes with one desire,
and incandesced a single fair.

*Because I do not favour lack
I do not wish on you worse luck,*
declared the restive billionaire
to foil the pauper's stony stare.

*Because I do not like how luck
and a moment's lightning lock
the roles of whipmaster and clown
I would not change your up, my down.*

This was the pauper's growled response
as both inhaled the scents of chance
and lived in small through our first million,
the neighbour impulse with reptilian.

And We Had Hands

(to the tune of 'Spanish Lady')

As I came down through Egomania –
(I wish I could recall the hour)
who should I see but a whisky matron,
stepping deftly from her shower.
Fluffed and orange was her towel,
dishevelled was her silver hair,
and in broad measure she showed pleasure
to find my ego naked there,

dangled, brangled, moistly tangled,
– lovely was her powder smell.
She walked her tigers through my jungle
fed them on crème caramel.

As I came back through Gaucherie
about the time when I was young,
who should I see but that feisty matron
catching raindrops on her tongue.
She smiled at me, her eyebrow lifted,
clinging were her azure skirts.
Those raindrops she both flicked them, licked them
like they were flirty extroverts.

And we had hands that would go handling,
clothes grown see-through round each limb –
such limbs to kick the moon to kindling
in blue lagoons where we would swim.

As I came down through Self-regard
and shed the glad wrap of my selves
who should I see but that rapt lady
calling to heel her timber wolves.
She trusted me to scarve her shoulders,
her creatures snoozed below our bed.
The Milky Way, like appliqué,
was coverlet for our instead

where we crooned tunes of rub and sidle,
with clerestories of license there,
illumined toil so sweetly idle
as earthenware felt earthenware.

As I came back through mortal coil,
a silver bushfire in my head,
I could not find my whisky matron,
neither our bed of Sweet Instead.
Bright pools of Ego, Gaucherie,
had hid their moonshine on our sea,
and yet that lovely whisky matron
thrilled me with her constancy

in reaches of my mind whose idling
flood-and-ebb took fine delight
found timber wolves and tigers sidling,
angels to our real night.

Her Lovely Stepping Out

(to the tune of Percy Grainger's 'Molly On The Shore')

Then I'll step if you step
and hair will sting our faces
where sea-blue darkens cloud-blue,
for we dance in breezy places.

So are your fingers in my hair?
Have I got skilful feet?
Why is the sand between our toes
so cold despite our heat?

Wé stép, gáles blów
from Reykjavik to Derry
And fingers dance on ivories
where quickness is not hurry.

Tresses sting and feet are white
where melody is devious,
Can I step ín where you step óut
or will my steps be previous?

Wé stép, clóuds shréd,
tides are on the shove
and melody must track its shift,
in ebb-and-flood of love.

Susurrus and susurrus,
the North Sea kicks its spray
to dance when time is clock work
and to dance when time's away.

The wind rears up its curlyhead,
there's pattern in a shell,
and toes that squeeze in sand have got
brief footholds that will tell

of melody's insouciance
to cast itself away
within the very sorcery
where it's habitué.

Maidenly

'Solveig's Song' from *Peer Gynt*

Sulur is the mountain above Akureyri in Northern Iceland where my mother grew up. The word means 'shawled woman', in Icelandic.

The Akureyri girls are out on Sulur.
   The midnight sunset's pallor
whites each 1940's pinafore
in which they gather the ripe blueberries.
And Mum, so maidenly, here you're othered,
your English years to me ungathered,
   and do you wonder what you're for?

Preposterous Captain G. has come.
   Your loveliness knocks him sideways from
his English puddings, Baptist regimen
that underlight this Oxford gentleman,
   who fresh from Blitzkrieg France,
now mauls Icelandic to decode his hopes
where girls are chattersome on Sulur's slopes,
and war so oddball in his circumstance.

Maybe there's song that steals up fjord and ness;
   to gleam and slide with inwardness,
let's say Greig's *Solveig's Song*, as it ascends
these pastures where the township ends,
and you, now cherished by your township friends,
   could not be more immersed in *North*.
   How might pure song, free-vowelling voice
trick your need for further earth
   and stranger choice?

How might a local girl transcend
   her localness to quit a friend
if not by music wildly cued
to offer her its amplitude,

music on its wavelengths making strange
    where memes and cells impel exchange
    in air outlandishly renewed,
    this charm, in-dwelling in deep space,
that gives to strangeness its inchoate face.

Atom and atom clinch to molecule
    to trick from time its inmost impulse,
    What else is here? What else, what else?
Atom, bridegroom, bride, the purposeful
takes Sulur down to favour Dehra Dun,
    first of your army habitats.
You've wived a life of never-fixed-address.
    Your photos home show Hindu dress
and Colonel G. bedecked with sundry cats,

    as Mum, you sound the opportune,
finding pals in *amah* and *kaboon*,
and colonels too, for friendship was your good
to seize how someone else's feelings stood.
    Five decades on, while raking leaves,
    down you go from heart. You made good lives,
good motherhood, yet still, what were you for
so whited on that hill in pinafore?

When someone raking leaves goes down from heart,
she goes from life that has no counterpart,
    and ditto every speck that's caught
    in any midnight sunset's net,
to go the way it finds, not where it ought
    like a woman, vowelling melody
finds the free flow through necessity.

Flambeau! Flambeau!

(to the tune of 'Nancy Whiskey')

Flambeau was the heart of ruby,
Flambeau warmed inside my head.

I was callow, I was show-off,
cosied Flambeau when she flowed,
let her take me from my schoolroom,
quick companion down my road.

Flambeau bronzed across the rooftops,
Flambeau lazy in my bed.

Lucas Windfall played his fiddle,
dancers ran before my eyes,
Flambeau led those carefree dancers,
gave to each their brief disguise.

Flambeau eased how I might parley,
Flambeau lit my shy Instead.

I went talking in the kitchens,
saw Roethke dancing with his dad,
Flambeau trailed her lovely shirt tail,
found for him his fatal bed.

Flambeau tremor through the neurone,
blue lacquer on a swimming pool.

I went walking with the whiskies,
Dylan Thomas sang his swag.
New York wowed his eloquence,
and found for him his body bag.

*Flambeau, mischief-maker in
the provinces of insulin.*

For forty years I've been a dancer,
learned the gestures of the dance.
When Flambeau pools on my small dance floor,
still she casts my nonchalance.

*Flambeau honeycombing moments,
lightning flash of my unsaid.*

Lucas Windfall

Lucas Windfall quit his cradle,
took with him his sherry fiddle.
I met him where the river flowed
and woke into the trance he bowed.

Lucas bowed a slanting deck,
I hornpiped on it for his sake
and leapt so high in that no-place
the stars were snowflakes on my face.

Lucas played me to the harbours
where his tunes drew cut-throat neighbours.
Our silly chins wagged at the sky
as Lucas played his hush-a-bye.

Lucas bowed a merry girl,
warm afternoons of sexual marl.
The streamers from his fiddle string
could prompt delicious tangling.

Lucas bowed a deeper reach
where I could dance but had no speech,
to tell what I could recognise
when my true love returned my gaze.

A violin will tease excess
from riffs of sheer exquisiteness
where Lucas Windfall is not idle,
conjuring liquid sense from fiddle.

Tudor Song

Lucas Windfall led me on.
In our bright plumage, like two swans,
we played the seigneurs by our lake,
behaving like we owned our luck.

Akimbo, Lucas said to me
*You'll have a cheap celebrity
unless some headsman holds your eye,
and you outstare that gravity*

*to coldly see our lives in small
and that this spoiler's falderal
is where the lightness of our style
must show the humour in its steel.*

We went dissembling through the town,
played rebel verb to rabble noun
where consciences in heron-grey
gave commentaries on our blasé.

A headsman's axe has edge and face,
his scaffold is a lonely place.
But petty deaths brought us to squalor,
filched the light from our high colour.

Yet Lucas Windfall showed me nerve
in just that tact of suave reserve,
that let me know I owned my luck
as swans draw light upon their lake.

Lucas In The Firebox Glare

Like one believing lies he quits his love.
Seagulls blizzard in the galley-trash.

Her presence was the only sea he longed for,
now sea-mash tucks its petticoats away.

She drew his shore-leave conversation suavely,
recalled with oaths now in the fire-box glare.

Her patience haunts him like a troubled outset.
A ship will leave a city like a spy.

If he were whole he'd swim the seas to her.
Every coastline spreads its jewelled arms.

Today comes lit by newspapers and liquor.
He knows the future by its hairline fractures.

He knows his Lucas-luck, his Lucas-alias,
blind particles that home upon *what else,*
    what else, whatever else.

Lucas Dogfox and The Violin

Fiddle, fiddle, slow your pace,
you'll have my nose outstrip my face.
You'll have the hairs that tip my ears
perceive the grinding of the stars.

Fiddle, hiccup and I'll sniff;
your reels of tune are my what-if.
I'm Lucas Windfall, alias fox
we lope together in our mix.

    Fiddle, when Lucas was a fox,
    he courted daybreak's shotgun cracks,
    for what's a countryside but ears
    and appetites in bleak arrears?

    Fiddle, when Lucas passed through death
    a nonchalance composed his breath.
    for fur and viscera composed
    no whole-of-mind where Being housed,

    but took him through death's little fuss
    to come upon the Universe.
    Time spinnaker'd away from him.
    All-being was his synonym.

Fiddle, hit-and-squeal death's wallop,
but still my parts lope at full gallop!
And I'm dispersed through every shard,
yet how to live this? That is hard.

Inis Oirr
(Barry Phillips on Cello)

Now here's a cello prises chill
between a collar and a hat,
and what we hear is lean and churl,
and where we are has no whereat

but islets maybe on dark water
where a ferry butts the spray
and strings of living sway the welter,
that's burnished with the ores of day,

these tussocks brushed like brassy hair
by a wind that grows immense
above the barns and cattle here
where cello rules the present tense

for such inchoate sarabands
where dancers in their firelight,
locate the joy in their grave rounds,
the complex code of their delight.

This code is ours, yet as remote
from life as is an hour ago,
seizing music's brilliant mote,
its tender touch and brutal flow.

Fiddle Music

Three fiddlers, turbaned like three mullahs,
compose light airs to lift the moon.
Their fiddles glow with saddle colours;
it's moonrise by our dark lagoon.

O we can coax this orange disc
to rise on whimsicals of air
and shine, our night-sky's asterisk,
highlighting buttons of who's here,

these loiterers, philanderers,
and slanderers with catch-all ears,
these silhouettes of gondolas
poled by English sonneteers,

these wedding guests with buckled shoes
who toast their groom, a cosmonaut,
this suave Jane Austen with Ted Hughes,
both skolling whiskies by the quart.

Our fiddle strings can make miaow
that infiltrates your quays of sleep
to mingle what was Once with Now
that brings the steeliest to weep.

*Once license fiddling in your brains
and you'll shape light to form from sound
in process that will ascertain
how time that runs is time that's round.*

Three fiddlers frocked in velvet coats
go squeezing cantilever tunes.
Exquisite their impromptu notes,
outlandish their uplifted moons.

Getting The French

Mister Shakeshaft with his eyebrows,
got the French into our fibres,
Dictée! Dictée! Point! Virgule!
in inkwell days of boarding school.

Mister Shakeshaft, mischief sniper,
shooting chalk at any gaper.
Gulp! *Alors, vous conjugez?*
Le professeur est trés fâché!

Mister S. in crowblack gown,
a-swirl with Gallic verb and noun,
was this a teacher or a nimbus
burling through our mental chambers?

His French is lodged, and his éclat
was a kindly, fierce *voilà*,
and such a gift that when he smiled,
it was first morning of the world.

Getting The Latin

Midders, Midders, Magister,
lead us through the conjugations.
Suffer our imperfect, sir,
to scritch like sea-caves of crustaceans.

Mister Middlebrook from Durham,
kindly and most dour of gents,
scowl away our harum-scarum,
neutralise our impudence,

for *crepitamus, crepitare,*
we creak, we crackle and we clatter
down the language estuary
absorbing all your arcane matter,

and Orwell Field is frosted satin,
the mercury is minus five,
first lesson up is double Latin
a Nissen Hut the she-wolf's cave

where Jim Wild cracks his knucklebones,
and soft percussion takes the desks,
and Durham scathing for these nones
growls 'Shoot oop, bebbis! Do yer tasks.'

But Midders, in the summer term
you read us Owen, and Sassoon,
so tenderly as to affirm
that dour and kindness are one tune.

So Midders, Midders, tight as scansion
in your belted gaberdine,
lead us to the last declension,
dunk us in the long Unseen.

Matron

The World is dark one inch ahead
What's on the other side?
Ted Hughes

Irma Geddon, Irma Geddon,
it's lightsout time and skies are leaden.
You count us one by one to bed
then tuck us in and shake your head.

We rode our bikes beyond the garden
to your displeasure, Irma Geddon,
found there the downslopes of Excess,
the shires of Moral Wilderness,

pedalled home happy, overwrought,
and spared your feelings not a thought.
Then dark came down and it was sudden,
just as you warned us, Irma Geddon.

Now weather fronts come raining nails
and runny noses gleam like snails,
and it seems queer, O Irma Geddon,
how your joys grow while ours must deaden.

We thought we had the rascal nous,
to match you, Matron of Bleak House,
and mocked your rack of plaited whips
called 'Gotcha' and 'Apocalypse'.

Now, you're among the beds and prowl,
attending whimper snuff and howl,
'My darlings, how your eyelids redden,'
you croon to soothe us, Irma Geddon,

and make us mindful, nightwatch friend,
how schooldays soon are at an end,
tomorrow with its big exams ...
'And no-one passes those, my lambs.'

And we are both your joy and burden,
your past and future, Irma Geddon.

Athlete's Foot, 1960

Miss McNeil could turn deaf ears
whenever Allchin tanned the rears
of after lights-out pillow-fighters,
and yet she sat us sinful blighters,
purpled the skin between our toes,
dealt out our socks and heard our woes,
we nascent Englishmen whose rears
now sit downstream of our careers.

We Boomer Boys

We boomer boys were once The Noise but now we run to trouble,
no longer seize those victories we scored when we were able,

as x-rays blaze arthritic ash where hip and thighbone groove
like heavy metal musos giving choir prac a serve.

And bio-mass beside our beds grows capsules, powders, ointments,
retirement ceding time at last for medical appointments.

We Boomer Boys went tertiary, degrees in feeling sore,
our liberal arts the scratching posts where undergrads might claw.

We Boomer Boys wore corduroys and styles of fustian flaunt,
for every style will catch the light before it turns aslant.

Here's *Beaky Mick*, whose maths was quick, who slowed himself on booze,
lived high on others' money and it little mattered whose.

Here's *Garry Sneer*, who gained the ear of critics in New York.
O deaf one, how's the buzz as you still ape the smart-set talk?

Here's *Col The Comet's* flash career, its focus and its verve;
the debris of his friendships showing highpoints of its curve.

Here's *Petit Moi,* whose self-regard proceeded jauntily
from Swagger Bluff to Hobble Lane on Cloud Hyperbole.

We Boomer Boys still find the ploys to star in raw statistics
for all our prime slot lifetimes were a lesson in ballistics,

one epoch shooting us to affluence's *Notwithstanding*
how present times will scratch for funds to staff the wards we land in.

What was it gave our boyo-eye its lightning derring-do?
When life became a fuck-up, who lived high on blaming who?

Titanium Where My Hipsters Rub

(for Doc Michael Gillespie and his team.)

I kept my two Icelandic hips
    through infancy and Uni.
They walked and bucked with witty loves,
    both medallist and looney.

They served through my home-making years
    a soccer parent's frolics,
or lugging babes and bricks upon
    synovial hydraulics

Then came my time of cartilege,
    my deeply personal hobble.
Masked surgeons disinfected knives
    to probe that gyro-wobble,

and nursing teams with their regimes
    to rebuild buttock muscle,
came gliding wards with sprightly words;
    I heard vocation's bustle

direct me not to cross my legs
    or gyrate on my pelvis.
Goodbye to my Mick Jagger days,
    Hello to Dalek Elvis.

They sent me home, I healed, and praise
    blue nous that gathered round
my drone of pain, reminding me,
    life points to the unfound.

Kindling The Real Estate Pages
(Energy can neither be created nor destroyed.)

Igniting a journal's pages,
   the flames glow green.
   No bytes or gauges
   measure my scene

as polymers of print
   soft-tongue the black
   in reach and feint
   on firebox back.

The Big Bang blew this thought,
   atoms combine,
   let all consort,
   not all will shine.

Closed systems and their perks
   make lives from heat,
   convert to works,
   this strangest feat

to move, be pent or glow.
   I am not zero
   if cosmic flow
   makes me brief hero.

A bloodline's like a star,
   it warms near-space,
   will warm so far,
   then ice its face

because its energy
    must deal elsewhere.
    So what is free
    if nothing's spare?

A people do their works
    then turn their speech
    into self-hex
    to shrink their reach,

ignite a journal's message –
    tongues luminesce.
    If all is usage.
    what grows less?

O Ignis Spiritus
Hildegard von Bingen

I hear a voice and voice, then counter-voice,
and these flow lake as dawn or gleam-of-stone,
to field suggestions from our universe
how voice might find a value, each its own.

Here is a flow, and here a counter-flow,
where voice is small in its immensity,
when plainsong lights beyond the light we know,
where abstracts live in physiology.

Small birds flow upward on their furious wings,
and yet their spiral's calm as it is wheeled
sunwards on their autumn journeyings.
I saw this happen in an English field.

So closure light that voice and counter-voice
to lume how pure is singularity
when utter dissolution is our choice
yet spirit tries its physiology.

www.ingramcontent.com/pod-product-compliance
Lightning Source LLC
Chambersburg PA
CBHW020336170426
43200CB00006B/410